Where
HUMAN RIGHTS and MENTAL HEALTH
interact

A Collection of Monologues
and Other Writings

TSL Drama

Published in Great Britain in 2020
By TSL (Drama) Publications, Rickmansworth

Copyright © 2020

Images courtesy of https://pixabay.com/photos/human-rights-prison-jail-imprisoned-3251000/

ISBN / 978-1-912416-38-7

Rights of performance

Contents

Age Guide

A monologue which didn't quite make it to the anthology is

Affirmations by William Sutton - you can find it at

Scottish Mental Health Arts Festival where it was performed in 2019

https://www.mhfestival.com/70stories/554-11-affirmations

Remembrance Day

by

John Samson

Setting

Jamie, a man, late eighties.
Jamie sits in a wheelchair, his legs covered by a blanket.
He stares at the ceiling.

Performance time:

10 minutes

Lights Up

God, I remember that ceiling. Spent hours staring at it.

He looks round the room.

The rest of the place is different. There were beds – cots really – a row down that side and another down there. Some more – the chronic cases – over there in the side chapel. There were no pews, of course, just the cots. And they would creak if you moved the wrong way. The worst was late at night when it was all dark and quiet and then someone would move and bang! That creak was like a bloody shot going off, a sniper blowing someone else's brains out. It would set the youngster in the end cot off, start him screaming. The nurses would be quick, by his bedside in seconds. They knew the screams put us all on edge, dragged us all back into the hell of the trenches. I would have to grip the sides of my cot whenever the screams started just so that I didn't go over the top myself. Where's Diane? Get Diane to him, she's the only one who can calm him down. She was the only one who could calm any of us down. The other nurses tried, bless them, but they were inexperienced women just trying to do their bit. They tried, but they could never truly hide their revulsion at the mutilation that littered those cots.

He pauses, looks down at his knees and gives them a rub, then shakes his head.

Diane was different. She came from the countryside, farming stock. She was used to the blood and guts from slaughtering animals. And she carried those fresh country smells with her.

He takes a deep breath.

This place used to smell of fresh paint, disinfectant and trenches. That trench smell clung to us all, closer than those sterile blankets we had to try and keep us warm. The other nurses would wear cheap perfume to try and overcome the stench of war. Take a deep breath, you can just about smell it here still, an under-note to the smell of hymn books and religion. But Diane …

He takes another big breath.

… she had the smell of open fields and sunshine.

He looks round the building again.

I suppose being in a church building I should have felt something, some sort of reverence or something like that. Mum would have wanted me to, she was a good church person was mum. But I couldn't bring myself to feel. When you've witnessed hell, it's hard to imagine heaven.

He subconsciously rubs his knees.

Good of the congregation to give over their church though. They had just finished building it, not even had a proper service, but they gave it over as a hospital for the war effort. Still smelt of paint.

Pause.

The nights were the worst. Nothing but blackness and memories to deal with. I would feel myself going, would try and cling to the sides of the cot to stop myself, but the memories …

He shakes his head, but the memories keep coming.

'I'll take care of him, mum.' Tea and buns. I wanted scones, but Davey wanted buns. He was the youngest so buns it was. 'I promise I'll take care of him, mum.' Sticky buns and scalding hot tea. Davey always got his way.

Pause.

Got a gutful of shrapnel too. 'I'm cold Jamie, so cold.' God, I thought he was going to die in my arms.

He stares off into the distance for a while.

Diane would save me. She and her fresh smells. 'It's okay,' she'd tell the other nurses, 'we won't be needing morphine now will we, Jamie?' She was good was our Diane. You didn't need morphine if she was there. You forgot your pain when she came. And we needed her … I needed her. Especially when that kid kicked off in the end cot.

Pause.

I wonder what happened to him. Just disappeared one day.

I would ache for the morphine. Not so much for the physical pain …

He rubs his knees.

… but for that hazy numbness that it coated my thoughts with. It blocked out the memories. But they had to ration it, didn't they?

Pause.

'I'm so cold Jamie.' He got hit did our Davey. It was bad, blood everywhere. To be honest I didn't think he would make it, not with all that blood. 'I'll take care of him, mum.' Boy, did that promise haunt me.

He looks round the building again.

I remember them filing in through that door, all the well-to-do old women. Wives of the Generals, I suppose. They would come in once a week to 'boost morale', do their bit for the war effort. Rally the troops and all that. I suppose I should have been grateful that they deigned to mingle with us. Brought cakes sometimes, but never as good as mum's scones … or sticky buns for that matter. They did their duty, but I could see in their eyes their disdain for the working classes. We were just coarse soldiers trying to escape the hell of the war, those old dowagers could never stoop to our level. So we played our little charade every week. The nurses would hide the worst cases from these women. Put a curtain round them, or give a bit more morphine to the kid in the end cot to prevent him having any screaming bouts.

'Yes, mam, much better, thank you. Oh, just me and my mum. Dad died in a factory accident when I was three.'

I kept Davey from them. He liked the simple things did our Davey – sticky buns and hot sweet tea, not posh scones. Not posh women. I would not give them the privilege of puffing their chests out in pride at a fine young English lad who raced across no-man's land to pull two of his mates to safety. Davey was not theirs to have. Got a gutful of shrapnel for his efforts.

Pause. Then resignedly …

I'll take care of him, mum … but the blood.

Pause.

They managed to patch him up. I thought he was a goner, but they fixed him up good and proper. And gave him a medal. Mum was as proud as punch. Little Davey with a medal. I've still got the photograph of her by his bedside when they presented it. Proud as punch she was. 'They melted down the shrapnel from my gut to make the medal'. Davey was a joker. Melted down the shrapnel to make a medal.

He shakes his head and chuckles, then looks around.

Diane will be back soon. She's aged some since those days, but still a fine woman. She was never a stunner like some of the other nurses. I'm sure those others have lost their looks, grown old and wrinkly, but my Diane never lost the smell of the countryside. She's kept me sane over the years, helped me through every remembrance service.

This chair creaks, you know. Just like our cots used to. I make a point of shifting in my chair in the middle of the minute's silence. A shot at dawn, fired deep into the heart of that silence that I hate so much. I don't want to remember. I want to forget.

Pause

'They melted down the shrapnel from my gut to make the medal'. Davey was a joker. But they sent him back as soon as they could. Sent him back into that hell with his gut all neatly stitched up and a medal pinned to his coat.

'I'm fine,' I would lie to those old ladies who came to boost our morale, 'just a stab of pain, but it's passed.' And they would nod kindly as if they understood. 'Oh my mum is fine. She makes a mean sticky bun.' They liked that. They could relate to that, go away thinking what a lovely young man I am who praises his mother's baking. They never knew Davey. I would let them have the sticky buns, but not our Davey.

Melted down the shrapnel from his gut to make the medal. But then they took that medal and melted it down to make the bullet to shoot him with. You can't keep your medal if you run away from the hell that tore your guts apart. They call it Post Traumatic Stress Disorder, PTSD, nowadays, but back then it was desertion. God, I hate Remembrance Sundays, the silence does my head in. Davey was the lucky one, he doesn't have to remember.

Long pause, then with a shake of the head:

I'll take care of him, mum.

He stares back up at the ceiling and the lights fade.

The Tracks

by

Tyler Texeira

Setting

Sitting reflecting.
Ethan, 17 years of age.

Performance time:

4 - 5 minutes

I often like to visit the old train tracks in the woods. They look pretty run down, like they would crack and break at the slightest touch, but they never do. A train runs along the track each day and nothing happens to the rails. The train is heavy and the tracks rattle much. It makes you want to close your eyes and cover your ears, but I've learned not to. It's better to hold your breath and not show that you're scared or worried. When you know the track won't break and the train won't derail, it's easier to feel safe. I don't feel that way anymore though. I know that the track can rattle, I know it can break, and I know the train can derail. I've seen it. And I couldn't help but close my eyes.

Pause.

All it takes is a simple crack. I didn't expect my mom to get sick. She seemed healthy enough. Sure, I had heard about breast cancer before. All the pink ribbon and three day walk Instagram posts. Yeah, I always felt bad but I never really thought about it much, it all felt distant enough. It sucked when I first heard the diagnosis. I didn't want to think about what it meant, but that was hard. I tried to distract myself, find new things to do and people to hang out with. I didn't always make the right decisions. It was impossible to forget when I was at home though.

Pause.

My dad didn't take the news very well. He would always get really angry and scream, even though there was no one to blame. My younger sister would get scared a lot. Sometimes it would be different though, instead of yell he would cry and hide in his room. He never wanted us to see him like that, but I saw it a few times.

Pause.

I would never tell my friends about my mom. All I wanted was to be normal, but I knew they wouldn't think my mom, or my family, or my life was normal. I think that was the reason I started going to the tracks. I felt like I had to pretend around my friends but hide what I was feeling around my dad and sister. I could let it all out at the tracks. Eventually though I didn't have to show any emotion on the outside. That's probably why I didn't cry when she died.

Pause.

But the rails in the woods never break. It always seems like they will but they never do. It's easier to feel safe when you know the train hasn't crashed before. I mean, it feels like it might crack every time the train goes by, but you know they won't! They never have and they never will! I guess that's what makes it so scary though, you never expect it. So you have to learn how to hold your breath.

Fade.

Class Participation

Jacinta Das

Setting

High school classroom

Elliot, an intelligent high school freshman whose academic performance has suffered since his sister's death.

Performance time:

8 minutes

Lights up

Hi. I'm Elliot. I didn't really want to come up here, but Dr Williams said he'd fail me if I didn't. Now, I'm sure most of you are wondering why the guy who's perpetually failing English is standing at the front of an English classroom. Trust me; I'm wondering too. Hell, do you guys even know who I am?

Maybe that's why I'm up here. Because I haven't raised my hand once this semester, and Dr Williams says the only way I can save my grade is through class participation. Basically, I have to stand here and open up about myself because that's what English is. Communicating about the human experience.

(*Looks at Dr Williams.*) Right? Okay, here goes.

So the prompt I chose is "describe your favourite memory". I chose it because I thought it would be the easiest, because, to be honest, I don't have a lot of good memories. I figured it wouldn't be hard to pick a favourite. One contender was my eighth Christmas and getting an Xbox, because that was the best winter break ever. Or my thirteenth birthday party, when Maria Wilkins, the cutest girl in middle school, had kissed my cheek during laser tag.

Looking back at it, I realise how silly I was. I thought I had become a man that day. When I got home, I ran upstairs to tell Lyssa. She was in her room, on her bed, reading a book, like she always was. Her door was slightly ajar, like it always was. Only later did I realise that she left it open for me, so I could slip in and tell her about my adolescent world. My big sister cared, even though she didn't always show it.

"Guess what, Lyssa, guess what?" She usually played along. "What? What?" She'd respond, and the excitement in her voice was genuine. Sometimes, especially on nights before exams, she'd seem preoccupied. And then I'd say something teasing –

18

like, "Oh, so you don't want to know?" And she'd insist that of course she did, she was just stressed, that's all. "Okay, well I can tell you another day then," I'd say, and that always got her attention.

That night, Lyssa closed her book, saying, "you'd better tell me, Elliot, or I'll never listen again." So I did, I told her about laser tag, and about Maria's sweet breath. I told her about the goo she left on my cheek, and was that normal? Lyssa had laughed, because it was lip gloss, and told me to be glad it wasn't pigmented. Otherwise it might've looked like a hickey. "What's a hickey?" I asked, and that made her laugh too.

Lyssa liked to laugh. I don't quite remember when she stopped laughing. I was fifteen and had more important things to do than sit around talking to my big sister. Besides, she was never home anyway.

She was in her first year of college, and she was always in class or with her boyfriend. I didn't like James, and I don't think Lyssa did either. Sometimes I'd hear her crying in the bathroom when she got home, way after Mom was asleep. I don't think she knew I could hear.

It became a sort of routine. She'd get home, lock herself in the bathroom, and cry. I never knew what to do, so for a while I didn't do anything. Eventually, she started running the bath water. I thought it was to muffle the noise, because she was embarrassed about the crying. Eventually, I worked up the courage to talk to her about it. I approached the bathroom door and was about to knock when I heard the retching. I froze and waited a few minutes for it to stop. But it didn't. She kept retching and retching. Thinking she was sick, I decided to leave her alone.

The next night, I approached the bathroom door and heard it again. It sounded like she was dying, the way she retched until she was gasping for breath. A few weeks later, we learned about bulimia in health class. We didn't go into detail though. All I knew was that it was bad. I didn't know how bad.

My favourite memory is of the night I knocked. I went up to the bathroom door, and knocked. And Lyssa told me to go away, and I didn't. I just stood there until she opened the door. Her hair was pulled back into a messy bun. Her eyes were red and puffy, her face streaked with mascara, and she reeked like puke. I didn't know what to say, so I just gave her a hug. Afterwards, she brushed her teeth, and got into bed. And I got in beside her, and we talked and talked until Mom woke up five hours later. I'll never tell anyone what was said that night, but I promise I won't forget.

I can't say how glad I am to have knocked on that bathroom door, to have had that one last long conversation with her. The next day, we resumed life as usual. Lyssa asked me a few times if I wanted to go out and do something, but I was busy with school and soccer, and I'd always put it off. And then one day she didn't wake up. The doctors said it was cardiac arrest and that it wasn't uncommon for bulimics.

Mom was shocked, said she had no idea that her daughter had an eating disorder. I pretended not to know too.

For a while, I thought it was my fault. Because I had known. And I didn't do anything, I didn't tell anyone.

I didn't even make time for her, and maybe if I had she would still be here. If only I hadn't been so busy. If only I had realised how bad it was getting, if only I could've gotten her to stop. It took me so long to forgive myself. But I don't blame myself anymore. Instead, I'm grateful that I had the courage to knock, to see Lyssa when she was ugly and broken. And I'm proud that I had the courage to love her like that, even when she had nothing left to give. I think that's what it means to be a man, to be able to laugh when it's easier to cry, to be able to love when it's easier to leave. But, hey, what do I know? I'm failing English.

Jess

by

Sue Hampton

Setting

21 year old woman

Performance time:

11 minutes

Lights up.

Now that it's happening, the beginning seems a world away. Partly because I'm not fourteen any more – I'll be twenty-one this year and that feels older than it should. And partly because we're one human family at last – give or take a few rich rebels – and at the start I was so alone.

It was November 2018 when I "met" Greta Thunberg in an online sense. I heard one of her speeches and it changed the way I looked at everything. And the way I had to be. She'd been spending her Fridays sitting outside the parliament building in Sweden for a while, with a CLIMATE STRIKE placard propped up against a wall. She looked younger than she was, with her plaits and her I-don't-care-about-fashion clothes. She was small. And her face was dead serious, because why would she smile about a climate emergency? I knew a bit about the science but at school and on TV adults only ever dropped in the phrase climate change as if it was no big deal, just a kind of inconvenience to flowers. Even the IPCC report only made headlines for a day, when the BBC told us we should eat less meat and use public transport. Then everything went back to normal. But not in my house. I can't un-know things once I know them and thanks to Greta, now I knew what she knew.

I decided before I told anyone. Then I explained to Mum. It was meant to be calm and rational but it came out in a tumble and my voice cracked. "Oh, I don't know, Jess," she said. I stared. Didn't she understand? "I'm more of a rule-keeper than a rule-breaker," she added. I reminded her that I hadn't had a deten-tion in my life and the most-used word in my school reports was "good". I said I'd write the letter and deal with the consequences. "What about your friends?" she asked. I shrugged because I couldn't speak for them. At that point Dad had only moved out about nine months earlier. I knew he wouldn't approve but I emailed him anyway. *This is a very serious step to take,* he replied. *I couldn't condone jeopardising your future with your exams on the horizon. We need to talk about this.* I replied that the world leaders and corporations were jeopardising THE future of our species – and the others we hadn't already managed to kill off – and if they didn't stop, and take action, any number of A*s at GCSE would get me nowhere. He said I was over-dramatising the situation so I said, *Read the IPCC report, Dad.* I didn't expect him to, but that Thursday evening he called me. "You have my blessing," he said, and he sounded choked. "Have you persuaded anyone to join you?" "Not yet," I admitted. Maybe I didn't try hard enough. I think I reckoned that if Greta had started alone, I could do the same.

Next morning was a frosty one in the village. My school was in the nearest town so I layered up and started walking with my CLIMATE STRIKE placard. On the back it said, THIS IS AN EMERGENCY with the Extinction Rebellion symbol and CLIMATE ACTION NOW. I figured I'd make an impression on the rush hour traffic and up my body temperature at the same time. When I arrived outside the Council Offices only a couple of streets away from school, I sat down on some cardboard I'd folded up in my backpack, and if other students went past me I pretended I hadn't seen them, just like most of them pretended they hadn't seen me. Some boy called me a geek and a few cool girls in Y10 looked down on me in more ways than one. Of course some people didn't know I was there but I counted on word spreading fast. My friends Shaz and Luke made a detour to see me. They were open-mouthed, as if I'd just stuck KICK ME on the head teacher's back. I wondered whether I embarrassed them. "How long will you stay out here?" Luke asked. "Will you bunk off

Maths as well as History?" "Maybe," I said. "This matters way more than any lesson." I got Shaz to take a picture of me for social media, hoping Mum and Dad would retweet – and Greta might be pleased to see me.

That first time was hard – like the ground. Before long my lips thought I'd had an injection at the dentist's. I almost wished I still had my puppy fat. The trick is not to think about what time it might be, or hot chocolate. I tried to stay focused on why I was doing it. Eventually Mrs Harris, my Head of Year, came out in her coat to see how I was doing. "I'm supposed to be encouraging you to come back to school," she said. "I don't think you can," I said, a bit squeaky by now and not too far from tears. "I respect your commitment, Jess," she said. "But you've made your point. It was a very good letter." "It's not about me, though," I said, as she hurried away.

Soon after that I checked my phone and found it was nearly eleven so I'd managed two hours. And people were liking my tweet, and telling me *Go Jess* and *Bravo*. I got up, a bit stiff for a fourteen-year-old, walked to school and signed in like any other student who was late. In the book I wrote CLIMATE STRIKE as my reason. Then I made my way to Science, hoping the teacher might let me explain the only data that mattered. But he didn't. Walking into the classroom I might have been a ghost. And in a way, I felt like one, as if I'd been somewhere the others didn't want to go or hear about.

I told myself it was a start. Some of my friends did ask me about it – "Weren't you freezing?" and "Will you get detention?" – and later that day Mrs Harris caught me in the corridor to say that if I was willing to talk about it in assembly she might be able to get me a slot. "Please!" I said, panicking because addressing a few hundred critical teenagers might make my two hour strike seem like a breeze. Mum didn't say much when I got home but she'd shared the photo on Facebook with the caption: *I'm very proud of Jess for her stand and very sad that she had to take it.* That made me a bit weepy when I hugged her. I think my parents both hoped that was the end of it, job done. But the next Thursday afternoon people at school were telling me they'd join me in the morning. It was just Shaz and Luke in the end, plus a Y7 called Barney who is meant to be a genius and had a better head for the facts than me, but it felt exhilarating. When we returned to school later that day a couple of Sixth Formers found me and asked to interview me for a podcast.

By the end of term our strike wasn't the only one that had grown. It was starting to go global and once Christmas was over, the growth was exponential. One day in January, 30,000 students marched in Brussels – and the next day I sat in the snow with eighteen students from my comprehensive, nearly as many placards, two primary school kids and their mums. And a dad. Mine. He was last to arrive and looked a bit stressed until we hugged. "I've been reading how Greta Thunberg insisted her parents stopped flying and went vegan," he told me half an hour later, when he had to go back to work. "Don't even think about it." "Dad ..." I began but he interrupted. "I ate my last bacon sandwich this morning. And who needs the Maldives or Bali when you can have Dartmouth or St Ives?" I told him the Maldives would go down before long and he seemed shocked, but not disbelieving. I didn't know then how soon I'd be proved right.

So much has happened in those seven years. Record temperatures, forest fires, floods, droughts, storms. Maybe it was Venice going under that made the difference. Or maybe it was us. The young ones. The rebels who wouldn't stop striking and marching and sitting down in roads until our leaders stopped failing us and took action. Only for years they wouldn't. They kept subsidising fossil fuels and trying to mine and drill and expand airports. Everything that would send emissions spiralling. But we kept on too – until every capital city in Europe and plenty in Africa, India,

Australia and the States was brought to a standstill by kids with banners and picnics.

Dad said it would never happen and our demands were too ambitious. He couldn't imagine governments giving up power. But I sang him a song I'd learned in Parliament Square: "If you want to know where the power lies, turn and look into each other's eyes." And I told him what sortition meant. That was how the People's Assemblies were formed, and in the UK we weren't too far behind Sweden, Denmark, Finland and Germany. No politicians with vested interests to corrupt thinking, just regular people of all ages and backgrounds. People who saw sense and chose survival of the species over profit.

Is it too late? Mum thinks so, I can tell. I don't know for sure but I won't give up hope. We've lost a lot – not just Venice and some Pacific islands but species my kids will never see. If I have any, which isn't likely, not while their future remains in doubt, under threat. People have dropped down dead in a heat humans weren't made to withstand. So the grief and the loss are built in and I think, that first Friday, I knew that already. But the madness has stopped. The climate criminals – including prime ministers, presidents and dictators, oil and coal execs and frackers – are behind bars and their assets are funding change. We're working together at last, the people of earth. There's no guarantee the seas will stop rising and I sometimes think about that poem, *Not Waving but Drowning*. I'm scared; everyone is. But we're one human family at last. How else can we save ourselves? You could say it's tragic that it took climate chaos to knock a sense of justice into us. But we're wiser now. Love's the strongest thing I know – apart from Nature, and we're making peace with her.

Dad says we'll pull through. Life is simpler. It feels more real. Is he right? Ask me again in another seven years. If we're still here.

Lights fade.

The Palliative Care Nurse

by

Heather Duthie

Setting

A confused 46 year old woman is dealing with the recent loss of her partner, a male nurse (Chris), whom she met at a rehabilitation hospital. She met him when her husband (JD) was admitted after sustaining a terrible injury which rendered him a paraplegic when a tree fell on him at a school sports day. The school where the accident happened is the same school where her/their children attend, and the school where the woman teaches piano part-time. While JD was in rehab, for over a year, the woman began an affair with Chris, eventually running away with him.

After Chris died, she became desperately lonely looking for love in some of the people close to her. During this time she developed a friendship/relationship with a close friend of Chris', and the story goes from there.

Performance time:

12 minutes

Lights up.

This sucks.

Do I really have to put into words what's going on in my life right now?

And why can't I keep some of the friends I made in this process?

She didn't come to see me yesterday and I knew she wouldn't . . . why? Because she wasn't exactly sure WHY she was coming to see me.

She came up to me at the funeral and passed on her condolences and told me how remarkable I was. And then somehow promised to come see me the following Thursday.

The night before I had some conflicting emotions . . . After all it is LESS THAN two weeks since he passed. The last 12 days of his life were the most full-on experience, traumatic and yet beautiful at the same time, watching a man slowly disintegrate before me and his friends by his bedside swapping stories from his life. A man???? You fool, he was YOUR man.

She knows my story. I told it to her the day I said my final goodbyes to Chris. I told her the whole story, including the bits Chris never told her, or anyone else for that matter.

And she stood there looking into my eyes and listening. And at the end she said, "I don't judge" . . . which to me means, "I judge". I don't care if she disapproves. Because, just as back in 2012, I'd rather be hated for what I really am, than loved for what I'm not.

That was that Friday. She said she would ring Monday to find out how things were. But of course she didn't. He had passed and she would have heard that along the way. It got to a few days before the funeral and I rang her to let her know the details of the funeral and then we had a nice chat. All the while me thinking, why am I telling her this, when I know her role in my life is officially concluded?

Do I worship her like I used to worship the male nurse all those years ago? Do I see her as better than me? Not hard, considering I see everyone as better than me.

And so when she didn't arrive that day, I wondered if I had missed her. After all, I was out having coffee with the only single male friend in my life. And there's another story. I am enjoying his company immensely. In fact, I was a bit late getting back to my place, hence me wondering if I had missed her. I didn't manage to get phone credit that day, because I guess my priority was getting all the gardening done, whipper-snipper, weeding, mowing, sweeping . . . all with the help of him and Mr Hostings.

So, then I decided to take in the donations from the funeral to the hospital. Somehow I managed to get to talk to some of the people from Palliative Care, and it was really nice to see Antonio, what a lovely man (in his 80's I reckon), even gave me a hug and I gave him a memorial card with the pic of Chris on the front, I told him where the photo was taken, Bombay Bicycle Club December 2012, the first year we lived together.

(*Side note.*) Remind me to attempt to get his name removed from Internet site for Nurses Board, out of respect for him passing away . . . THOSE BASTARDS. Who are you to decide it's wrong or right if I want to begin a relationship with a new man?

I was taken up to the ward nurses station where I spoke to a couple of people, nurses, and then at my request they called her and she came up to see me. Big hugs and little chat, she asked me how things were going and I replied "a bit hairy, change of dynamics in relationships now that I am a single woman etc etc etc". We eventually began walking off the ward, arm in arm, MUST SAY I've never experienced that before LOL. At that time she said to me, sorry I couldn't visit as there were not enough cars. Interesting that she chose not to ring me to let me know, busy perhaps?

I gave that man everything he wanted. And now . . . here I am all alone. I knew this was coming, but you can't stop a runaway train.

Why am I desperately trying to cling to this friendship? It's not even a real friendship. It's actually a bit like the one with Katrina back in the day. We spent many an hour together, but it was her official capacity, and my free time, and in the end she moved away and our friendship ceased, after she inspired me to write many songs . . . I don't like feeling like this, vulnerable, needy, unworthy. I feel like telling everyone to fuck off so that I can be left alone in my misery and not hope to have any happiness whatsoever in my life.

(*Checks Facebook/phone to see if he's written her any messages.*) This life really sucks.

What's happening? I know things have to change but do I not get ANY joy or pleasure in the process? After the nightmare of living with a terminally ill man and burying him and losing my "vocation", for want of a better word, surely I could be forgiven for attempting to find intimacy again? Life HAS to change now, why am I to be condemned if I suddenly become involved in another intimate relationship? And what about this bloody mole on my shoulder blade? . . . that should actually be my number one priority, everything else is completely ridiculous if that turns out to be the big C.

Anyway we walked off the ward, talking, not noticing that the elevator had gone down . . . speaking of which, ask me about the other night. We went down in the lift and walked out of the hospital and continued talking and eventually we hugged and kissed and said goodbye, whereupon she said she would call in sometime . . . which is not going to work because I will be going away, as I am going stir crazy and feeling very exposed. I crave sex, because I know I can't have it, just like before with JD's accident. I crave it and feel I deserve it, and am in the aftermath of this bereavement business which has definitely increased my libido, so basically I'm a walking mess, there should be a sign round my neck, don't fuck the patient. WHEN can I have it????

Lights down

(***The following piece can be performed separately or added to the first part after a pause.***)

Winter's Bloom

(a brief essay on death and life)

Lights up

The thing about winter is . . . nights are longer, darker, colder.

We spend more time waiting for daylight and warmth than we do enjoying daylight and warmth.

They say don't plant flowers in winter . . . the ground is too cold and nothing will bloom.

Yet miracle of miracles, on Friday 26th July[*] a beautiful white flower bloomed in Northgate and the woman who noticed it thought of me and the day I was facing . . . a funeral. She

---

[*] Southern Hemisphere

wondered on the miracle of the flower blooming on the same day that my companion was farwelled at Mattiskes, and eventually sent me the flower as a memorial gift.

As far as farewells go, it was a happy occasion with many laughs, some completely unexpected, and some tears. But mostly many fond memories shared of a man who loved maybe just a little too much, definitely drank too much, and who always helped without hesitation.

Being such a funny man, whose impressions could not be bettered by anyone, everyone at the funeral wore colourful or even Hawaiian shirts. The casket was accompanied down the aisle to the sounds of Elvis Presley singing *Don't you step on my Blue Suede Shoes* . . . whereupon the Celebrant, Irene, got up and said, "well that was different", before proceeding to put on a Hawaiian shirt, over the top of her Salvation Army uniform, one of Chris' actually, and then started off the service.

Daughter and grand-daughter spoke and did him proud.

The photo presentation evoked laughs and tears accompanied by the sounds of Harry Connick Jr singing, *If they asked me I could write a book* . . . then Ed Sheeran singing, *should this be the last thing I see, I want you to know it's enough for me, Tenerife Sea.*

I got up and addressed the flower-laden casket saying, "Chris, since Sunday, they've got a new Prime Minister in England . . . Boris Johnson . . ." Everyone knows how that ended.

The service continued with three of his best mates telling stories of their friendship. Jasmine sang beautifully the song that Chris had chosen, *Think of Me* from the *Phantom of the Opera* soundtrack. Ben played *Close To You* on my nylon stringed guitar, the one signed by world-renowned classical guitarist Slava Grigorian, when he came to play in the Palliative Care Ward on Monday 1st July.

Mum, Major Irene Dean, closed out the service with a poem and then the service ended with a tune by Madness, *Oh what fun we had*, Baggy Trousers . . . and everyone milled out to the back room for coffee and talk, or tea, or biscuits . . .

Donations were collected to be passed on to the RDNS and the Palliative Care Ward, Nurse Sue, made it to the funeral and afterwards made plans with me to catch up soon.

Not long after that, most of the people went down the Slug & Lettuce, where we had our first drink in December 2010 – my invitation, to celebrate him with a few drinks . . . It was a great night catching up with quite a few people, and having a bite to eat. Greg was on hand to take photos, really good ones which I will treasure forever.

By 8.00 p.m. I was exhausted. It had been a heavy but, should I say, successful day. Wendy drove me home and we went practically straight to sleep.

Next morning we decided to go to TTP where she insisted I/we get our nails done, after dropping off at the local chemist the unused medications from the past final weeks of his existence. I asked if we could drop into Holden Hill music on the way where I picked up my beautiful new Tidepool green/blue Fender "Player Series" Stratocaster guitar, named Wallace by the Hostings, and Chris by Wendy LOL. Then we ate and came home again. Wendy went off to visit her brother and I played with my new toy.

HIM . . . H. I. M.

Around 6 p.m. Wendy came back, bringing nice Alcoholic apple cider cans with her to boot. Then HE came over, as had been arranged between him and Wendy at the pub the night before. We watched Netflix and YouTube and had a lot of laughs . . . It eventually dawned on me that the reason he had wanted to come over was to ask Wendy about his brother in Darwin . . . whether or not she knew his name.

I sat on the couch next to him and little did he know that in my heightened state I was having some confused thoughts, triggered by his nearness. I guess that stands to reason when you think of what I had just been through and what I had just lost.

SHE . . . S. H. E.

The next day Wendy went home via the airport and I don't know what I did. Oh wait, no, I went down to Semaphore to see my friend and her new surroundings. We walked along the beach before going back to her house to have a couple of glasses of wine. I met her daughter's lesbian partner who turned out to be a brilliant pianist, mostly playing by ear some fantastic pieces, such as Bohemian Rhapsody and songs by Billy Joel, who she clearly adored and told me the story of her interaction with him at his Adelaide concert. She was so excited.

Eventually me and SHE went back to her room. Again I was having weird and confused thoughts while being in an enclosed space with her. They began to manifest as I tried to help her with the music she was trying to play on her you-beaut speaker. She eventually said she really needed to go and help with the meal for her daughter. I apologised profusely and ended up getting under the covers to attempt sleep as I was exhausted. She came back eventually and we spoke again and I said maybe I needed to go get some counselling. I said I don't think I'm gay but I do have feelings for her. I went home.

HIM . . . H. I. M.

The next day I got in touch with HIM and found out he was at the RAH having a medical check-up. I offered him to come over for a coffee which he did eventually and we went out into the back yard to discuss the lawn and the ashes, eg where they would be placed. There was a hug.

Later that night I confessed to him via messenger the fact that I had purposefully avoided being alone with him in the past 12 months, as I had begun having slightly inappropriate thoughts about him and I was damn sure nothing was going to prevent or complicate my life as I looked after Chris in his final days.

He was blown away by what I said . . . in hindsight I probably shouldn't have said it, but I really did want to see where things stood between us. I was sick of all the second guessing, so even though I probably made a fool of myself, at least I found out that he was not trying to pursue me in anyway . . . it was . . . All . . . me.

At less than two weeks since his passing, I was raw with emotion and desperation and would have happily thrown myself at him if he would have allowed it . . . Thankfully, I guess? He didn't.

On Thursday, he and Greg came to help in the garden . . . Bloody marvellous, before Greg got there, he helped me with my blocked toilet and after Greg left we spoke for a bit longer.

Oh, I didn't mention that in the morning we had met at Beacon Lighting to help get him a refund for his sensor lights. Then we had coffee, then as we left I somehow disarmed him with some comments . . . After he told me to "be good, and if you can't be good, be good at it LOL . . . I had replied, "I'm very good at it" . . . LOL. He was confused, perhaps even a little excited. Who knows . . . ?

On the Tuesday, when he rang me to tell me that nothing was going to happen between us, he eventually invited me to help make soup at his place on Saturday. I assumed his mum would be there, as it was her recipe. I also thought his son would be there. When I arrived he gave me a peck near my lips and we proceeded to make the soup. This took nearly three hours, during which time his son arrived home unexpectedly. I think this slightly annoyed him . . . I didn't mind. His son decided to have a little drink and then offered me one. I reluctantly accepted, it was delicious. Then he left, and we carried on. It was a very enjoyable time but torturous at the same time. Eventually I gently "told him off" because he had broken my "new rule" in which I didn't want to be allowed to be alone with him, because of how it would make me feel. He apologised but not before confessing that he "thinks about me all the time". He also made a point of asking me about something that happened a few days before Chris passed away, when HE brought his mother over to visit Chris. He asked why I went quiet when Chris, after obviously having "lost his filter" . . . the cancer had gone into his brain by this time . . . Chris was trying to suggest that me and HE would, or perhaps should, get together, in front of HIS mum for god's sake . . . Of course I went quiet . . . I was thinking that she might be thinking I'm trying to sink my claws into her son . . .

We finished cooking the soup. I was allowed to have a little sample. Yum. He had to go out. We finished in the kitchen and then we went to the lounge to watch TV, *Frasier*. We sat in the two lounge chairs side by side. I only sat where he directed me to sit. We barely watched the show, but continued to talk, all the while having almost wholly unbroken eye contact.

When it was time to go we hugged for a bit longer, his arm did start to move slightly down my back but that was all. Then he told me I looked nice and colourful and my bag was colourful, LOL.

Eventually we went out into night where I said my goodbye and then quickly kissed him on the lips, came as natural as breathing. Then I left.

HELL HATH NO FURY ...

By

Jennifer Russell-Hawkins

Setting

Confident but extremely anxious female around 50 yrs of age.

Props: Crumpled sheet of paper. Mobile phone. Wristwatch.

SOUNDS OF car hooting and mobile phone.

Performance time:

4 minutes

Lights up

My cab will be here soon. I need to practise my evidence one more time before the hearing.

He may be the best in his profession; BUT he deserves what's coming to him.

I'm sure I will win. I was a vulnerable patient, taken advantage of . . . I need to be articulate but not over confident, in fact a little timid would be best.

I need to practise that more.

Yes . . . to be truthful I led him on. I'm not giving that in my evidence.

A year ago, I hadn't left my house for six months.

Every time I got to my front door, I shook from head to toe, couldn't open it.

We started the therapy by FaceTime. He was amazing, kind, understanding, gorgeous. After just three sessions, I was able to go from the house to a cab, to him, I've heard he's the best and I'm living proof.

We worked together for many months.

There was a connection; I definitely felt something and was on a high after each session.

I have this age thing and he made me feel I was still attractive and desirable.

In no time, I was back at work, MY CONFIDENCE HAD RETURNED!

And I was falling in love, I just adored that feeling. I never wanted it to stop. When he said that we had come to the end of all he could do for me . . . I was happy to be cured but devastated I wouldn't see him again.

He explained that I had now to rely on myself, not him.

I still can't decide if it was fate that our paths crossed that day at my niece's wedding.

He ignored me when I saw him in Reception: and then again, at the lift.

He was on the groom's side; a sort of usher. I started to feel my confidence slip, so many people, him ignoring me. I'd not felt this anxiety for a long time.

I checked my stuff into my room and got ready for the ceremony. Then I saw him again; he ignored me, AGAIN!!! Didn't even show me to my seat! I was fuming.

Even though the ceremony had started I held my mobile down low and texted my friend; her reply was immediate: "Professional etiquette darling, perfectly normal, don't take it personally."

How dare she, not a bit of support, what sort of friend is that?

After the ceremony, I hit the bubbly . . and in the break I followed him to his room: "Jonathan?"

He spun round looking embarrassed. I'd never called him by his first name before, "Why are you ignoring me?"

He touched my hand, I could see he'd been at the bubbly too. He said that he didn't think I would want to explain to anyone how we knew each other.

"Look I need to lie down, I've drunk too much."

I pushed my way into his room and within a second we were embracing.

Suddenly and forcefully he pushed me away.

"STOP! We can't do this, I will be struck off, go, please, go, go now!!!"

He literally pushed me out of the room.

I was furious.

It's my word against his. They don't like this sort of thing but I still need to be sure. (*Finds crumpled paper in pocket.*) Here it is, my evidence . . . it's so crumpled, I've read and altered it so many times, but it is right, now, I am sure. I will record it on my mobile and listen to it in the cab.

Breathe, deep breath.

(*Reads from the crumpled paper into mobile phone.*)

"I was surprised to see my therapist at my niece's wedding. He came over to me as soon as I entered the ceremony room and welcomed me. He told me how gorgeous I looked, which surprised me.

I know I shouldn't have, and I am truly sorry for this mistake, but I did accept his offer, for champagne in his room. He said others would be joining us.

I was the first to arrive, then after I had finished my glass I became uncomfortable as no one else had come. I said I was leaving. He tried to persuade me to stay, I said 'no' and the next thing I knew he was groping me and pleading with me. I pushed him away and fled in a dreadful state."

Perfect. That's it, that's my story. Straight and to the point. I can do it.

Breathe, slowly, stop over-breathing . . . in for four, out for eight.

(*Looks at watch*) . . . Oh my God! where's my Uber. I can't be late. I can't be late, I just can't miss this opportunity. Stop panicking, keep breathing . . .

I'm going to wait outside, that will save a bit of time.

(*Shaking from head to foot.*) I can't open the front door, I can't stop shaking . . . breathe, breathe, slowly . . . I can't, it's not working –

(*Sounds of – car hooting, mobile ringing . . . these noises keep on until the end.*)

I can't move.

Lights down

At

Stop the London Arms Fair

by

Leslie Tate

Setting

A person old enough to have been at the Stop the London Arms Fair.

Performance time:

7 minutes

Lights up.

Four young people were lying in the road, "locked-on" as partners. One pair had an arm each buried in a connecting steel tube, the other pair were linked by a large grey suitcase. Their "locked-on" arms, disappearing into solid blocks, looked like they'd been amputated.

It was eight thirty in the morning outside the ExCel Centre, East London. The "locked-on" couples were blocking the dual carriageway to the London Arms Fair. A queue of lorries and vans delivering weapons and display materials was backed up beyond the approach bridge. It was windy and overcast but the protesters were jubilant and the police had given up threatening to arrest anyone who stood in the road.

The woman on the ground by the central island was twisting side to side. She wasn't finding it easy. All four protesters had cushions under them, but lying there required mental strength to be surrounded by a wall of police with the certainty of a cutting-out process and arrest to follow. The locked-on couples were as exposed as patients in a dentist's chair, and only too well aware of their own helplessness.

The woman on the ground had a "health and welfare" colleague crouched by her, offering water, and a legal observer watching the police, while the other protesters were singing and calling slogans. It was stirring, uplifting but edgy. Unlike medicine there was no sedation and when the cutting-out team arrived – large men all dressed in black – the serious operation began.

It takes courage to lie flat on your back blocking large lorries. It also requires mind-control to stay calm while notes are taken and you're warned of arrest. It needs the kind of detached self-abandonment that stunt people practise. It's an act of imagination, visualising the children who will be killed by these weapons, and putting principle before safety. So it's about generosity, and driven by conviction. Most of all, it's unselfish and defiantly meditative. The trick is to give up control, look the other way, or see the dark humour in it.

The cutting-out team, like the police, saw it as a job. If they'd stopped for a moment they would have recognised the protesters were driven by the same impulse as them – the desire to protect victims and stop crime – but they chose the instrumental approach, using their technical skills to get a result. For them, morality didn't come into it.

For the woman on the ground the cutting-out process was a testing experience. Surrounded by black-clad men with power tools, and masked like them to protect from flying particles, she was wincing, partly in anticipation and partly in pain. To break through several layers of impacted material took a long time. Tearing and prising the suitcase apart was difficult and although the men in black handled it with precision, it was jarring and humiliating.

Afterwards, the woman passed from one captivity to another. She was handcuffed, charged and taken to a vehicle. The crowd applauded and cheered her all the way, then the police resumed their activities, threatening arrest, clearing the road and some vehicles passed through.

In the downtime that followed there were performances and speeches, people made craft models, sewed cloth, planted miniature windfarms, chatted or wrapped up against the cold. Despite news of two more lock-ons at the other gate, a trickle of traffic passed through largely unopposed. No one wanted to be arrested. Then suddenly, when the heart seemed to have gone out of the protest, a big lorry arrived and a group holding a blue silk banner stepped out. Several other protesters joined them and began to retreat towards the ExCel gate in front of the lorry, chased at a walk-run by the police.

It lasted a few minutes. The lorry went through. But when the police turned around they discovered their mistake. There, lying in the middle of the road, were a couple of young locked-on women with a suitcase between them. The decoy action had worked and the road was blocked again.

Arm-locked on tarmac
and fitted to her partner with a joint prosthetic,
the young red-headed woman
is here to block a truck.

Her body's her bond.
The softness of flesh, tubed in metal,
arms against war. Smoothed across
roughness, she's playing dead,
holding her ground on pock-marked asphalt,
in a dream of Montgomery and Stonewall.

To lie down makeshift hurts,
blurring the line between power and loss
as she spreads against the black,
moving side to side, and close to crying out.

When the men in gloves show up
it's an extraction.
They operate masked, picking away
with trained steel to hit those points of entry.

Their power is in doing. Tooled up
and giving out sparks, they surround her
with all-action drills to cut off her connections.

When they crack her from plaster it'll be in one piece.
They'll lift her in order from roadblock to pedestal,
held to account by a cheer.

Till then, on countdown, she is waiting.

Her cause keeps her there. Her roots go deep.

UCBs Talks

People Power & Water

By

Rachie Ross

Setting

Lecture theatre or outdoor podium/'soap box' stand
Adult

Performance time:

10 minutes

People Power

Lights up

People power; you can say that again! Power for good and power for bad.

In case we hadn't noticed, it's not the whales who are overfishing, it's not the polar bears who are melting the ice and it's not canaries who are flying with fossil fuels.

We certainly have the power!

Let's use our privilege and power for Godly Goodness.

In Exodus 1[*] we meet five powerful women who use their power to resist evil, stand up for the vulnerable and change history. This is the first example of non-violent-direct-action (NVDA) in the Bible. The two Hebrew midwives are told by the king of Egypt to kill the Hebrew baby boys at birth. They don't. Clever, cunning and cool they simply don't play ball. And God sees their bravery and honours them.

Then we meet Moses' mum who prays and prays and prays and puts Moses in his floating coffin and pops him on the river Nile, trusting God's power. She refuses to give into despair. She says no.

Then we see Pharaoh's daughter picking up the floating basket out of the reeds when she's out washing one day, and we see her look in and see a BABY. She doesn't see an issue but rather she sees a human being, a real flesh and blood baby. She refuses to follow her father's order and says NO to his murderous command.

And then, last but not least, we meet Moses' sister Miriam who was watching, waiting and was ready. She was ready to speak

---

[*] Sura 28, Al-Qasas, in the *Al-Qur'an*

up when the time was right. She offered a clever solution. Preparation meeting opportunity is powerful all right.

All five women powerfully resisted in their own way.

Each refused to take part in evil in their context.

Each said Not On My Watch!

Powerful people, seeing real people, not issues.

Let's not see climate breakdown as an issue, but see it as real whales, real polar bears, real canaries and real babies.

Let's be prepared to speak and act when the opportunities come, having deep courage.

Let's take every opportunity offered to us to defy and resist evil in our day.

Join us. The time to tell the truth is now. The time to Act is now.

Power to the people!

UCB1 talk - Water

Water, the wet stuff. A very good thing.

One of God's key building blocks of all life on earth; plants, animals, reptiles and birds, and we are a staggering 60% water. The pale blue dot we call home is blue because of water.

Water of life, sloshing and splashing and overflowing to bring growth, food, health and life itself. Think wells, taps and swimming in cool blue seas and bubbling brooks. Think "goodness". Think right water, right place.

Or water of death, raging, flooding and spilling, crashing over river banks, pouring over sea defences, flattening towns and villages. Think tsunamis, and New Orleans and Noah's Ark and hurricane Dorian. Think Destruction. Think right water, wrong place.

And then there's no water; dry river beds, empty aquifers, nothing to wash with and nothing to drink. Droughts, crop failure, emaciated people and animals. Think starvation and enormous suffering. Think wars for water and mass migration of people. Our Palestinian brothers and sisters in Gaza are due to run out of water next year.

It's about balance. Too much or too little water in the right and wrong places causes enormous problems as we know.

As we cause the earth to heat up, we disturb the water cycle. We will see **more** of too much water and **more** of too little. UK soils dry out too, OUR plants get heat stressed too and OUR rivers burst their banks; just ask the people of York, Tewkesbury, Lynmouth, I could go on. And that's without even mentioning sea-level rise.

Climate change is dangerously mucking around with the water cycle.

Can we hear God's earth groaning? Are we listening?

Do the tears of the poor need to turn to torrents before we say enough is enough to global injustices, one of which is water?

Local flooding and local droughts are but a drop in the ocean compared to the global seriousness of disturbing the water cycle, pun fully intended.

What Bubbles found when she was lost

by
Amna Agib

Bubbles, the fish, was so young when she got lost. She didn't plan a trip or swim around. She just lost her way. The waves took Bubbles far away.

Sometimes Bubbles felt suffocated, at others she found herself in dark and dirty places. The tiny fish was unable to identify her location or navigate the way forward, as if she lost her natural Global Positioning System (GPS). The current forced Bubbles to go in circles, causing disorientation and confusion to her system. The density of the water kept changing as well.

Bubbles had a very vague memory of a clean, crystal clear bluish water. It was different to that which she faced during the unpleasant, forced journey. She was trapped in unfamiliar different yet similar enclosures. It was not surprising that Bubbles didn't recognise the shapes and colours, which kept shifting following the change in the direction, length and strength of the waves. There was one similarity, which all the places shared, the inability to swim in a straight line.

When Bubbles was inside, she felt helpless and totally lost faith in reaching safety. Although she was certain of her sharp sight, she saw different colours in the various circular one-way lanes. Anyone would lose control there. The waves were not so strong inside to offer the required push forward. The challenge was how to find the only available exit, which seemed like the eye of a needle. It was the only hope and chance to escape the unknown. Nevertheless, it seemed like it was the ultimate cost you needed to pay to defend your freedom. Bubbles was subjected to a traffic jam situation, which was unpleasant. It was a very terrifying incident, especially travelling with a huge group, which you did not choose or know before.

Luckily, Bubbles was captured by some people who set her free from the lock-in scenario. Although anyone in her shoes, would thank God millions of times, yet Bubbles felt sad and uncomfortable, as she missed her home, family and community.

Bubbles discovered that there were many fish and sea occupants in the several tanks in that room. They tried to communicate, emitting various sounds, squeaks, whistles and croaks including vibrations and clicks. The atmosphere gave the impression of an orchestra that plays a foreign tune for the first time but nailed it. In addition, many species interacted by body expressions imitating sign language. For the workers, it was like a mural that united the sea life around the globe.

One day, they woke up to a sweet distant echo just like a melody created by light drops of rain on a slow-moving stream. It had an unwinding effect, which was badly needed. Behind that impression there were worries, concerns and enthusiasm as the sound became louder.

A group of children with special needs, were on a school visit. The children were warned not to tap on the glass, to avoid causing mental distress to the inhabitants, who were still resting. One tiny fish whose name was Bubbles, caught their attention. Her eyes were so sad but very welcoming. Maybe she remembered happy days, before the catastrophic changes she endured at the deep, blue end. Surely, she missed her school.

The teacher set a task for the children to guess why these sea species were kept here and not in their natural habitat.

"They usually live happily in the zoo, because people feed them."

"Miss, the place here is bright not like the deep end of the sea. They might feel scared when it is dark."

"They may have been washed away because the water is so shallow. We travelled to the coast during the school holiday. At the beach there was a lot of mud and just a little water. To be honest we only saw worms wiggling across the shore."

One of the older children quietly said, *"I have asthma. I learnt, when the atmosphere becomes dirty, I feel sick. My parents take me to the hospital. I guess when the sea gets dirty, their parents bring them here to make them feel better. Are you fish doctors?"*

"You are all right," said the woman who welcomed them at the gate. *"We look after you as well as them."* That was how Diana, the Sanctuary Manager, started her talk about the environment and climate change. *"Our responsibility is to preserve the environment."*

One clever boy asked about the connection between climate change and the fish in the tanks. Diana pointed at the girl who cleverly observed the declining water level. *"It is true that the water in many rivers becomes shallow."* Looking at the girl she continued, *"Although you only observed worms, we often capture some dying fish on the shore. You know fish can't survive outside the water. That is why we have this building. I suppose it is like a hospital as you said. Today you are learning about the environment and the impact of climate change."* She continued, *"The most horrifying fact is that we neglect our environment in the nastiest, uncaring way. Unfortunately, these beautiful sea creatures pay the cost."*

She then asked each child to name their favourite food which they enjoy when they are at the seaside.

A child replied that he enjoys ice lollies. Diana asked him whether he drops the plastic wrapper on the floor. With a wry smile he reluctantly nodded his head to confirm that he did throw it on the ground. Another one declared that he also leaves plastic bags, fizzy drinks and water bottles at the seaside. A girl added that she usually eats fish and chips and also leaves the package on the floor.

A pair of twins spoke at once. They said they like chocolate but their father, who is a fisherman, had never allowed them to throw any rubbish on the floor. He always said to them, *"Fish are our life, don't hurt them.*" He explained to them that the rubbish which people threw away, kills the fish.

They didn't quite understand that. One day they went with their Dad fishing but he caught nothing. At home they heard him saying they need to rent a one bedroom flat in a poorer district. For them it meant they will change their school and lose their friends. They still feel sad. As a result, they just hated fish.

"I am glad you disclosed that. I would like to show you a short film, before we discuss this topic further," Diana said with no hint or prejudgement.

The film drew their attention to the fact that the plastic bags and bottles were the same enclosures which Bubbles and others were sucked into. Diana asked the children why Bubbles saw different colours when she was entrapped. Total silence. She smiled and asked a couple of children to name the shop where their family buy food. Every one shouted louder with a name of a shop. Then Diana asked them about the colour of the shopping bags. *"White, orange, blue, multi-coloured,"* they replied.

"Do you now understand why Bubbles saw different colours whenever she was trapped in what the fish saw as closed one-way lanes?" All shouted at once, *"Yes miss. They were the multi-coloured shopping bags."* Diana continued, *"Although they were different in colour their effect, in the wrong place, was the same, strangling the fish."*

The child with asthma approached the fish tank where Bubbles was kept and said, *"We are sorry if you had asthma because we throw the plastics on the floor which made their way to the sea."* The twins did the same and whispered, *"We are also sorry for hating you for no fault of yours. On behalf of our class we are keen to help."* They definitely saw her smiling at them. They smiled back too.

In relevant and simple language, Diana explained to the children the impact of mistreating the environment. She informed them how volunteers, including divers, participate in cleaning the seabed.

"The rescued fish and other species are kept in the tanks in ideal environments till they are fit to go back. Freedom is the most precious right for everyone including our guests from the sea," she added.

The children were informed of the centre's programme of games for those who have different disabilities and the tailored activities for many organisations and schools.

Diana concluded her talk by saying, *"Some children who come to visit us may have felt lonely, sad or frightened because of a bad experience at home or at school. They may have no friends or are being bullied because they look different. However, following their visit, their mood improved as we encourage them to feed the fish or help those which were washed up on the beach. They usually do very well, as you did today."*

At the end of the session, Diana invited the children to enter the competitions the centre held during school holidays.

Clapping was very loud but, surprisingly, the tank's inhabitants were not distressed. On the contrary, a lively parade was displayed in support of sorting out the impact of climate change, to protect the future for the coming generations.

"Earth belongs to all of us," a sound came from all directions in many different languages and the screen exploded with sign language and large print writing. Soothing music was played with different colours slowly filling the room's environment with happiness.

Please let it be so

by
Nick Horgan

Characters

Young girl
Father

Setting

Indoors, a family home, a few years from now, a father and his
daughter are sitting together.
Clock in sight

Performance time:

10 minutes

Dad and young girl sitting.

YG: Daddy, what did you do in the climate protests?

Dad: I met your mum. And we sang songs. And we sat in the road ...

YG: You sat in the road? Isn't that dirty?

Dad: It was, but if we sat in the road then the lorries couldn't drive to where they were going.

YG: Didn't that make the lorry drivers angry?

Dad: Yes some of them, some said they'd run us over, and some of them said "well done mate, I've got kid's too, but next time give us some warning."

YG: So did you just sit there?

Dad: We did.

YG: And what happened?

Dad: The police came along and asked us to move but we stayed there, so they arrested us.

YG: Shouldn't you do what a policeman tells you?

Dad: Yes, but ... it's not always ... sometimes you have to ... you have to think about it the day before, that you might want to get arrested and go to jail.

YG: Did you go to jail?

Dad: Yes.

YG: And mummy?

Dad: Yes, she was sitting next to me, holding hands with me on one side and your uncle Andy on the other. Other times we were chained together with padlocks the police couldn't unlock, but that time, the first time, the plan was to make it easy.

YG: So it was okay because you were with mummy?

Dad: Yes, and we knew we had to get everyone to notice what we were doing so they would talk about it. We wanted to get on the news, not to be famous, but so lots of other people would see and want things to change too. You remember when you got your bike but you didn't want to ride it because you thought you'd fall off? And then your friend Amy came round and showed you she could do it, and then you gave it a try. It was just like that, if people could see we could do it, they could do it too.

YG: So that's why you were sitting in the road?

Dad: Yes, because we needed lots of people to join in the climate protest. We needed lots of people to do it so we couldn't be ignored.

YG: Why do you need lots of people?

Dad: If I sat in the road right now, on my own, you wouldn't join me. You'd think silly daddy, making his trousers dirty.

YG I'd stand on the pavement and shout "quick mummy's coming."

Dad: You would, you'd think "Daddy must be careful not to be run over." But because there were lots of us, and we had flags and drums and songs they couldn't ignore us and they couldn't run us all over.

YG: So it was fun?

Dad: It was fun but it was important too. We had to do it carefully and together. And it was worth it, because we stopped it, didn't we. Because we started something they had to take notice of,

YG: So what happened after the police arrested you and mummy?

Dad: We were put in a police van, with lots of other people who had been sitting down in the road, and we went to jail. We all had our own room, and we just waited, and at midnight they let us go.

YG: Why's that?

Dad: I think the policemen wanted to join in with us more than they wanted to arrest us – plus the paperwork.

YG: So you weren't angry with the police?

Dad: No, they were only doing their job, which is just what we wanted.

Two hours later.

YG: So Daddy, you know when you were sitting in the road with mummy, holding hands –

Dad: Yes?

YG: And you wanted everyone to notice –

Dad: Yes.

YG: Did they notice you? – Were you on television?

Dad: We were on the news programme, lots of times. And as more people joined in, it was on the news more and more. All the protests everywhere, all around the world. In some countries the police weren't very nice but the people didn't give up. When you're a bit older they'll teach you about it at school, how all the carbon in the air was making the world hotter, and how dangerous that was.

YG: Were you really on the television?

Dad: Yes, and mummy was interviewed one time about what we were doing,

YG: Mummy? Did she look pretty on the television?

Dad: Yes, and clever, pretty and clever because she had all the answers, she knew about carbon footprints and sustaina-

ble energy, and environmental vandalism and plastic pol-
lution. And how the poorest people of the world would be
affected worst. Whatever they asked her she could tell
them what was wrong and how to change it,

YG: Were you asked questions by the man on the television
Daddy?

Dad: No,

YG: Oh, why not?

Dad: Oh I think they liked mummy better because she was so
pretty and clever. If you want to get everyone's attention
then you can make a lot of noise like we did sitting in the
road, or you can speak clever sensible things that everyone can understand and agree with, and mummy is very
good at that.

YG: And everyone agreed with mummy?

Dad: Nearly everyone, in the end. Other times there were famous people talking about it, actors and politicians and
footballers and singers and eventually nearly everyone
was talking about it and asking the important people in the
government and the business to change things. And the
children in school were talking about it.

YG: We get told off for talking toooo much.

Dad: Well this was much naughtier than talking in class. Some
of the young people said, "this is important we want to
join in." But they had to go to school, and they weren't
allowed to get arrested. But they weren't happy that the
important people who make the rules weren't doing anything about the problem of climate change.

YG: So what happened?

Dad: The children went to school but sometimes on a Friday they would say we're not going to school because there's no point going to school if the planet is dying.

YG: It was dying?

Dad: It was sick and no one could make it better on their own. We all had to make it better together. So the children said we're not going to school on Fridays. Not to be naughty but to show everyone how important it was to them too.

YG: Did they get in trouble?

Dad: Some did, and some didn't because their mums and dads already knew it was important and agreed with what they were doing. And some didn't go to school because they really were naughty and didn't want to go to school anyway, before they understood about the planet dying.

YG: So can I not go to school some days?

Dad: If you have a very good reason, a very very good reason, like it's the day to save the world again, then it's okay. But if you do go to school you'll learn how to keep us safe and keep the world out of trouble for ever.

YG: So if I need to save the world I can miss school.

Dad: Yes, of course, but do ask mummy first.

Next day -

YG: Daddy?

Dad: Yes?

YG: Yesterday you said you were sitting in the road to get the important people to listen.

Dad: Yes, we wanted so many of us to get put in jail that they'd wonder what was going on.

YG: What was jail like?

Dad: Oh don't worry, this was the small jail at the police station, not the big jail where they send the criminals.

YG: And the police locked up everyone who was in the van with you?

Dad: It wasn't just us, there were lots more vans full of people like us, and on the news they said there were too many and the police had to stop arresting people because the police stations were full, at least a thousand people.

YG: A thousand people, all in jail!

Dad: Just to make the important people in the government and running the businesses see it was serious, and important. More important than them, which took a long time. The trees that clean the air were being chopped down, and where the polar bears live the ice was melting which made the sea bigger. You remember when we made sand castles and when the tide came in it was all knocked over? When the sea got too big that happened to real houses, and people died and some poor people lost everything,

YG: All because the important people wouldn't listen to you and mummy?

Dad: And all the scientists and the activists. Food wasn't growing properly because it was too hot, and all the insects were dying,

YG: Insects like flies? – You don't like flies.

Dad: Not just flies but the bees as well, and we need bees.

YG: To make honey, mmmm honey.

Dad: Not just honey, see the plants that make food have flowers and the special bits of the flowers called pollen have to be mixed up so the plants can start to make the food, like apples and potatoes and tomatoes. And because the bees are so small and clever they go buzzing from one flower to another to another mixing up the pollen from one flower with the next one. But if the bees don't do it the plants don't make the food.

YG: Bees go buzzing and have furry bottoms.

Dad: They do, but they were dying out.

YG: Why?

Dad: You see, the insects eat some of the food or spoil them, and lots of the farmers didn't want the insects around so they sprayed the plants with a poison that kills the insects, but then there weren't enough bees to mix up the pollen, and the poison was making humans ill too.

YG: So they stopped?

Dad: Eventually, and now the numbers of bees and the other insects that mix the pollen are getting better, and the food is better because some of the poison was getting in the food, and now it's not allowed.

YG: Good, because I don't want to eat poison.

Dad: Nobody does, but it took a long time to change the way the businesses grew their food. That was just one of the things that had to change.

YG: And it changed because you and mummy sat in the road?

Dad: Not just us, thousands of us, in the end. Because there were so many things that had to change. There were so many problems. Remember after Christmas we asked you to tidy your room because you had all your new things and the wrapping paper we saved and your toys out from when Emilia was here, really messy. And you thought it was too much to do and you cried, and you didn't want to because you wanted to play instead.

YG: There was so much messiness to tidy up.

Dad: And we helped you, and we tidied up somethings and then we went and played for a bit and came back and did some more, and together we did tidy everything up together.

YG: I never thought we could do it but we did it.

Dad: We did, and the planet was like that, too much to do, carbon in the air, and plastic in the sea, and people making things and then throwing them away and making more things the same and throwing them away, making a mess, silly really. Like when you made clothes with mummy for Molly, and you dressed her, and then when you made more, and more, we said you had too many and asked you to give some to your cousin, but you hid them under the bed.

YG: That was a good hiding place.

Dad: Yes but what if you had kept making things you didn't need and didn't share. Emilia wouldn't have any clothes for her baby and soon there would be no room under your bed, and your bed would lift of the floor and it would be touching the ceiling and you'd need a ladder to go to bed !

YG: So people were hiding things under their beds?

Dad: No but they were throwing them away, for someone else to find somewhere to put them, and they were still making more, and more. And you know when you make baby clothes there are always bits you've cut off left over, but we can't use them because they are too small.

YG: Mummy said they were too small to even make elf's knickers!

Dad: Rude.

YG: Rude!

Dad: So all the left over bits were making a mess too and it was all a waste because people didn't need to make so many new things because they already had too many clothes and phones and cars and shops and plastic bags. But they kept making more.

YG: Why? That's silly.

Dad: Because people were greedy. You remember how you felt when you wouldn't give Emilia those things, remember you said later you didn't like how it felt – greedy and selfish – like you were scared we were going to take them all away, that's how the people with all the things they didn't want to share felt. And there are poorer people all over the world who need us to share, and to pay them properly for the work they do for us, like sewing together our clothes or putting the inside of our phones together. There's enough for everyone if we share.

YG: We're sharing now aren't we?

Dad: We're sharing more, and helping each other with turning the waste into useful things. And the people who can't grow food are being given enough food and other help. That's what everyone has agreed. The people in charge now know that everyone wants to stop the climate change, and they have to do the things that will make it happen. And so far it looks like we've stopped making the planet more dirty and even hotter, and we've stopped fighting about it for now.

YG: That's good, isn't it?

Dad: It is.

YG: And there'll be no more fighting ...

Dad: We hope so ... we hope there'll be no more fighting.

Lights fade.

www.ingramcontent.com/pod-product-compliance
Lightning Source LLC
LaVergne TN
LVHW021545080426
835509LV00019B/2854